WORK SMART AND BECOME RICH

By: Takarudana Mapendembe

Takarudana Mapendembe is a qualified Biomedical Scientist with more than twenty years of experience in Clinical Biochemistry. Moreover, he is a businessman, a writer, and a cryptocurrency enthusiast.

CONTENTS:

INTRODUCTION

CHAPTER 1: Where to Easily Get Start-up Money

CHAPTER 2: The Five Biblical Money Principles All Wealthy People Follow

CHAPTER 3: Stop Giving Lack of Money Excuses For Not Starting Your Business.

CHAPTER 4: Don't Only Work Hard, Work Smart As Well.

CHAPTER 5: Real Happiness in Life

CHAPTER 6: How to sell anything to anyone anytime.

CHAPTER 7: How have you made money on the internet?

CHAPTER 8: Should you start up your own company or not?

CHAPTER 9: What are the most useful business startup ideas?

CHAPTER 10: How can I start freelance writing fast without experience?

CHAPTER 11: What's the best online business to start that doesn't require much of an upfront investment?

CHAPTER 12: How do people become rich at a young age?

CHAPTER 13: Can a religious blog be profitable?

CHAPTER 14: How can I start making money on the internet?

CHAPTER 15: How do small businesses get Instagram and twitter followers?

CHAPTER 16: How do people become successful?

CHAPTER 17: The Growth Stages of Venture-Backed Private Companies.

CHAPTER 18: Now you can play ball.

CHAPTER 19: 20 Jobs You Can Do With Just General Certificate of Secondary Education (GCSE) Qualifications:

CHAPTER 20: How to Revive Your Business After Lockdown

CONCLUSION:

INTRODUCTION:

"If you want to be successful, study, learn about, read about, and research on how successful people acquired and still manage to maintain their success. You, too, will become successful," my great grandmother told me when I was only 5 years old.

To help you and me achieve our goals in life, I have compiled a list of about ten best pieces of advice from billionaires. They are below:

1. "If you do things differently, success will follow you like your shadow, and you can't get rid of it!" By Sheldon Gary Adelson.

2. "You have the opportunity to go out and change the world in so many ways. Seize the day. The opportunities are there but you have to reach out and pick them up." By Steve Ballmer.

3. "Why will the customers want to pay you anything over a long period unless you are creating value for them? Long-term success starts with being dedicated to creating value for others." By Charles Koch.

4. "If you want to be a winner, then compare yourself to the best, and acknowledge that will never happen without hardwork." By James Dimon.

5. "Being an entrepreneur isn't really about starting a business. It's a way of looking at the world: seeing opportunity where others see obstacles, taking risks when others take refuge." By Michael Bloomberg.

6. "If you want to be happy, set a goal that commands your thoughts, liberates your energy, and inspires your hopes. It marks a big step in your development when you come to realise that other people can help you do a better job than you could do alone. No man can become rich without himself enriching others." By Andrew Carnegie.

7. "One of the greatest discoveries a person makes, one of their great surprises, is to find out that they can do what they were afraid they couldn't do." By Henry Ford.

8. "If you think you can do a thing or think you can't do a thing, you are right." "Failure is simply the opportunity to begin again, this time more intelligently." "The competitor to be feared is one who never bothers about you at all, but goes on making his/her own business better all the time." "A business absolutely devoted to service will have only one worry about profits. They will be embarrassingly larger!" By Henry Ford.

9. "If you want to succeed, you should strike out on new paths, rather than travel the worn paths of accepted success." "I do not think that there is any other quality so essential to success of any kind as the quality of

perseverance. It overcomes almost everything, even nature!" By John D. Rockerfeller.

10. Below is Lesley Brown's advice: a. "Someone's opinion of you does not have to become your reality." b. "Change your mindset because you don't get in life what you want; you get in life what you are." c. "Practise OQP (Only Quality People). d. "Develop your communication skills because once you open your mouth you tell the world who you are."

Work on these and you will be successful. However, please always keep in mind that success is not the accumulation of wealth or riches, but it is the achievement of your own goals not others'.

CHAPTER 1: Where to Easily Get Start-up Money

So many brilliant disruptive business ideas, inventions and innovations are never acted upon. Some of them get started on but die as soon as they start. They end up being buried at the cemetery soon after their owners die. This is not only caused by the fear of failure but more so, by their owners' lack of sufficient startup money. This must not happen to you and your ideas in this day and age because there are now so many places to easily find startup money.

Thomas wanted to start a buying and selling the business but he did not have enough capital. He wanted to buy items from liquidation companies, auctions, wholesalers, manufacturers and car boot sales and resell them on eBay, Amazon, his own shop and his own website. The capital he needed to start amounted to about $10,000. Thomas had $1,000 in his savings account and he also had two credit cards with a total of $2,000 that he could withdraw. He borrowed $3,000 from his bank and $4,000 from family and friends.

Within two months, Thomas had the $10,000 startup money he needed. He started his business two years ago and he has already repaid all his loans and credit card debt in full and he is one of the top sellers on eBay and Amazon. Thomas was very lucky. Some people do not have any savings at all and neither do they have credit cards. Others do not have rich friends and family to borrow money from and most people have their loan applications rejected by banks. However, these days of internet technology there are many different places where you can easily get business capital.

I know some people who got money through some television shows, for example, Shark Tank, Dragon's Den and The Apprentice. To get funding from billionaires in these shows you need to have a very good business idea with a working prototype. You also need to know your business competitors, your cash flow, your market and future growth. It's very competitive but you should give it a go. You can also get business capital in the form of a low-interest loan from [Virgin Startup](#). They give startup loans to new entrepreneurs. The loan amounts range from £500 to £25,000. You can also get money from angel investors and venture capitalists and they can be found on the [angel investment network website.](#)

The internet is a great blessing that came to humanity. Nowadays you can easily raise business startup money on crowdfunding websites like [Kickstarter](#), [Indiegogo](#), [Seedrs](#), [Funding Circle](#), [Companisto](#), and many others. On some of these crowdfunding websites, you give your product to your funders in exchange for their money and on others, you give them shares. Some of those crowdfunding websites also give loans which you will have to pay over a certain period of time with a low interest. Do your own research before you pitch your idea so that you decide on what's suitable for your business first.

If your business project is a blockchain one, you can easily raise startup money by doing an initial coin offering (ICO). There are so many blockchain projects that are raising millions of dollars through ICOs. The ICO Drops website has got active, upcoming and ended ICOs. An ICO is almost the same as an initial public offering (IPO) except that in an IPO people buy company shares and in an ICO people buy tokens which they can hold onto and sell later at a cryptocurrency exchange for a profit.

I hope this will help you to easily get that needed startup money for your business and make you bring your best disruptive business, invention and innovation ideas to life sooner than later.

CHAPTER 2: The Five Biblical Money Principles All Wealthy People Follow

All wealthy people, be they Christian, Atheist, Buddhist, Muslim, Mormon or Traditionalist, follow five biblical money principles every day. They may not know that they are following these principles. Some of them know about them and how to continue following them but they don't know that the principles are biblical.

One theologian told me last week: *"The Holy Bible is the best oldest economics, finance, and accounting textbook ever written. From Genesis to Revelations, it's pregnant with accounting, finance and economics data, facts and lectures. If you follow them, you will become one of the wealthiest people on earth, but if you don't follow them you become poor and miserable like everybody else. Whenever you lose whatever you have in life, just follow the biblical money principles and you will bounce back."*

I can hear some people saying: *"How can the Holy Bible have money principles? My Pastor tells me that money is evil."*

Your Pastor is selfish. He/she is not being generous with the truth. Yes, The Holy Bible has got money principles in it and in this article, I give you five of them. Every wealthy person follows them daily and if you follow them every day, you will become wealthy, too. However, this is not a get rich quick scheme or one of those *"don't work hard, or get money for doing nothing"* scams. This is the opposite. It requires you to work very hard day and night.

You must have a written budget

Luke 14:28–30 says: *"Suppose one of you wants to build a tower. Won't you first sit down and estimate the cost to see if you have enough money to complete it? For if you lay the foundation and are not able to finish it, everyone who sees it will ridicule you, saying, 'This person began to build and wasn't able to finish.'*

Before you get paid, it's important that you write down a budget and strictly follow that budget after you get paid. I know some people who are very good at writing a budget every month but come payday, nobody follows it. There are many people who don't write down a budget at all and yet they say they are devout Christians.

A budget tells you what you are going to use your money for. It helps lead and guide you towards the achievement of your goals. It shows you where you are coming from and where you are going financially. It tells you where your money comes from, where it goes and what you spend most of your money on. Without a budget, money comes in and leaves you before the end of the month without you knowing where it's all going to. That is why most of those people earning money only twelve times a year always have too much month at the end of their money.

Avoid debt

Proverbs 22:7 says: *"The rich rule over the poor, and the borrower is a slave to the lender."*

Let's say you happen to be one of my friends who like to have a brand new car every five years all of them being bought using a car loan or lease scheme, and $450 of your hard-earned salary goes to the loan or lease payment every month. If you work for forty years doing this, the total amount of money you paid to the car dealer will be $216,000. That means for forty years, you have been a slave to your car dealer and you gave him/her a total of $216,000 for enslaving you. I say this because whenever you did not have enough money you suffered from fear, stress, and depression caused by fear of having the car taken back by the car dealer if you miss payments.

Always surround yourself with quality people

1 Corinthians 15:33 says: " *Do not be misled: 'Bad company corrupts good character'.*"

So many people destroyed their careers and businesses by surrounding themselves with people who did not have the same diligence, desire, faith, enthusiasm and the will to succeed as themselves.

I know so many people who are always pessimistic about almost everything they do, everything that happens to them and everything that does not happen to them. They always look at the negative side of every situation. If they get money, it's not enough, do something good for them, they say they didn't need it done anyway. Play with them and you will end up being the same as them.

Some people never keep on working hard towards the achievement of their goals in life. They give up. Why? It's because of the company they keep.

Play with drug addicts and you will end up being a drug addict. Hang out with lazy people and you will become lazy, too. Play with successful people and you will be successful. *Birds of the same feather flock together.*

Save and invest

Proverbs 21:20 says: *"The wise store up choice food and olive oil,
but fools gulp theirs down."*

If you invest $500 per month in an investment that pays 5% interest per year, and you invest it for forty years, at the end of forty years you will have about $747,802.29. Your total deposit will be $240,500 and a total interest of $507,302.29. If you had just done that for twenty years you would have $205,055.54 in total. Your total deposit would be $120,500 and a total interest of $84,555.54. All wealthy people invest money.

Wealthy people also save money for a *'rainy day'*. There are always *'rainy days'* in life. The car breaks down unexpectedly. You or your loved one gets ill and they need an operation. You get injured or ill in such a way that you won't be able to work. The boiler needs fixing. The boy next door kicks a ball onto your bedroom window and breaks it. All these and many other situations that unexpectedly happen to people need money. Where will you get it from if you don't save?

Be very generous

Proverbs 11:25 says: *"A generous person will prosper; whoever refreshes others will be refreshed."*

Psalm 112:5 says: *"Good will come to those who are generous and lend freely, who conduct their affairs with justice."*

Giving makes you feel happy. Just the thought that you have willingly given something to someone who needed it makes you feel different from how you felt before. It also opens the doors for more opportunities, miracles and satisfaction in your life. By giving you are attracting blessings from GOD.

Conclusion

Follow all these five principles daily starting from now and you will see your life changing positively. By this time next year all your friends (the ones you hang out with before reading this article) will be asking: *"How did you do that? How can we turn our lives around the same way you did?"*

CHAPTER 3: Stop Giving Lack of Money Excuses For Not Starting Your Business.

All profitable businesses require capital. This is the money and/or other assets that you need to start a business. Sometimes it may be very difficult to get capital. However, there are various types of businesses and their capital requirements differ. Some need a lot of startup money in tens of thousands or even hundreds of thousands of dollars whereas others need only five hundred dollars or less.

Selling on Amazon and/or eBay:

I asked a friend of mine, Johnson, how he started his business, and he said: *"When I started my online buying and selling business last year, I only had $200 in my savings bank account, a laptop computer, broadband at home and my smartphone. I registered on eBay and on Amazon as a seller and listed some of the things that I no longer needed, for example, my old books, used phones and unwanted gifts. Within a week, I sold all and got $100. Now the problem was that I had no goods to sell and for a week I did not sell or buy anything. I was looking for suppliers.*

"Lucky enough, after exactly seven days of inactivity on my eBay and Amazon stores, I watched a video on this dude who bought Amazon customer returns and other goods from liquidation companies, picked them up himself with his own

car and then listed them for sale on his own website, on eBay and on Amazon. He also sold some of the goods in his own bricks and mortar shop. I fell in love with this idea and bought two pallets on Liquidation.com for $300. I picked them up with my car so that I could save on shipping costs. Soon after picking them up, I took pictures of them in my garage at home and listed them on eBay and Amazon. Within less than a week, they were sold out and I made a profit of $1500."

He continued: *"I continued buying goods from liquidation companies, local auctions and car boot sales and I'm still doing that. Now, besides selling on eBay and on Amazon, I also sell on my own website and in my shop. I started this business a year ago and now I am earning more than $10000 net profit every month."*

There are so many ordinary people who started their own businesses the same way Johnson did and they are now millionaires. However, everything in life has got advantages and disadvantages. I interviewed twenty eBay and Amazon sellers and they had this to say:

Advantages of selling on eBay and Amazon:

Online marketplaces like eBay and Amazon have got very high traffic. You can start your own e-commerce website today but you will have to spend hundreds or even thousands of dollars every month just to sell less than ten items whereas on eBay or Amazon you don't have to spend money on advertising.

Customers are there already. You just list your product with a very good description and high-quality pictures and within a day or less, it's gone. eBay has more than 164 million active buyers and Amazon has about 184 million visitors per month.

Amazon executives say: *"Sellers report on average 50% increase in sales when they join Amazon Marketplace."*

Furthermore, you easily acquire new customers because people visit eBay and Amazon in search of products and once they discover yours, you are in big business. If your products are of the highest quality and sold at a low price, you get new customers every day and those customers keep coming back to you for more.

Many people prefer shopping via marketplaces, be they online or not. Marketplaces have got various products all in one place and that draws a lot of customers. Online marketplaces have got single stream checkout and fulfilment support as well.

Disadvantages of selling on eBay and Amazon:

Amazon and eBay charge marketplace fees. They charge you for listing your items for sale and they also charge you a certain percentage of the selling price after the product is sold and this may dramatically reduce your profit levels or even tragically leave you with a loss depending on the type of goods you are selling and their profit margins. It's very good and advisable practice to do your maths before listing.

Do you know that when selling on eBay and/or Amazon you have got limited control over your business, it's growth and direction. They restrict branding of your own presence. They restrict the communication between you and your own customers and they also dictate what items you can and cannot sell. It's their platform, not yours. They are in it to make money. More money than you. That's why Amazon is blamed for identifying popular products, stock them themselves, ban you from selling them and they sell them themselves.

If you have got your own e-commerce website in addition to eBay and Amazon stores, keeping inventory in sync can become a nightmare to you. Your own shopping cart and that of the online marketplace don't sync making it difficult to track and understand stock levels without a lot of manual reconciliation.

Selling on Etsy:

Betty, a mate of a friend of my cousin brother's mate told me about how she started her business on Etsy with just her smartphone without a computer, money in her bank account or broadband at home.

She said: *"A friend of my uncle's girlfriend introduced me to Etsy. She had heard that I was very good at making jewellery and I made her and her husband's wedding rings. They both liked the rings and since they were family friends I did not charge them anything. She told me that I could make money selling my handmade products on Etsy. I registered a seller account the following day and listed three rings I had made the month before. Within a week they were all gone and the customers left very good reviews. I then made some more rings, necklaces, earrings, bracelets, to mention but a few. I started this business three months ago and last week I quit my nine to five job as a nurse to focus on my business because it now pays me more than twice the amount of money I earned as a nurse."*

Etsy is an online marketplace for handmade products like paintings, crocheting, sewing, crafts, etc. The advantages of selling on it include the opportunity to sell your handmade crafts, the opportunity to sell craft supplies if you want to be a supplier and if you can easily and cheaply get your hands on the supplies in bulk, the opportunity to sell ebooks on patterns, crafts and tutorials. Furthermore, Etsy has lower fees than other online marketplaces. Moreover, they have got training courses on how to run your Etsy shop.

However, the main disadvantage of selling on Etsy is that they do not allow you to sell mass-produced items.

Samson, my uncle's best friend started his business on eBay and Amazon with only his smartphone and mobile data as his capital. I asked him how he started it and he said: *"Five years ago I heard about dropshipping and studied it for a month before starting my business. I started my business using only my smartphone and mobile data to buy goods from manufacturers and wholesalers and then resell them on eBay and Amazon without handling any stock or dealing with postage and packaging. That business made me a millionaire."*

Dropshipping is a type of business whereby you provide goods by direct delivery from the manufacturer or wholesaler to the retailer or customer. The advantages of this business model include: it's easy to get started, there is no need to manage stock or organise inventories, expansion of assortment, it's easy to scale up or down, it allows you to operate on a very low budget, it allows you to have a healthy cash flow, you don't need a website as you can sell on high-traffic online marketplaces like Amazon and eBay, and there is no risk of a bad buy that results in overstock issues.

However, with drop shipping, it's not easy to find good, reliable drop shippers that do not serve thousands of other sellers and you don't control anything except your prices and the products that you offer. In addition to this, there are potential quality issues, risks in offering and selling products that are no longer available from the drop shipper resulting in potential customer service issues. Moreover, the drop shipping market is now overcrowded with thousands of other sellers selling the same product on the same online marketplace, for example, eBay and Amazon resulting in very low margins.

Even though you have got very little or haven't got any business startup money at all, with just your smartphone and your mobile data you can start a business and succeed. You just need the strong desire to do it and the unwavering faith that you will succeed no matter what.

CHAPTER 4: Don't Only Work Hard, Work Smart As Well.

"You have got to work hard to succeed," has been and still is a number one song sung to all kids by their parents almost every day all year round. Hitherto, numerous multipage books and articles have been written about working hard yet many people including you and me work hard, but only a very small easily countable number become really successful. Why is that? How does this work? What brings in this massive difference? Where does their real success come from?

In an attempt to find some answers to the above questions, I asked my nephew, Lewis, a high school headmaster and he said: *"There are three categories of students. We have got the lazy ones who never do their homework and/or assignments and they never read books. They just come to school because their parents force them to. Then we have got the hard-working ones who are always reading, memorising and cramming. The third group is comprised of the smart hard-working ones who aim to understand everything their teachers teach them. This group is the cream of the school and they excel in almost every subject and in sports, too."*

His answer reminded me of my days at high school. We had those lazy people who always copied assignments a day or a few hours before the submission due date or time. Then there was this heavy dude who always memorised whatever he read and went around the school dormitories chanting whatever he had crammed. The smarties took understanding everything in the syllabus as a priority. The smarties are now doctors, scientists, accountants, successful business people and writers.

I still remember two of my best friends, though. They were Aloise and Godfrey. Aloise was very hard-working. Every time I saw him, he was reading. He had no time for jokes, playing, let alone dating girls. Almost every day, he read his books till late at night and woke up very early in the morning to read again. He never entertained any disturbance, loss of time and discussions with classmates.

Godfrey read his books only during the stipulated boarding school study times. During his studies, he focused in such a way that if you ever wanted to draw his attention or disturb him you would have to loudly blow a trumpet into his ear. After the study time, he played hard. Furthermore, most of the time people saw him go to the teachers to ask questions. He also discussed school work with his fellow students.

What surprised me between these two fellow students is that, whereas three months from exam time Godfrey started making strong friends with the syllabus, past exam papers and teachers of every subject, Aloise never did that. He kept on working very very hard, reading day and night and cramming whatever he could not understand.

Come examination time, Godfrey passed with distinctions and maximum totality in all subjects, but Aloise only managed to pass half of the subjects and failed the other half. Aloise worked more than 50% harder than Godfrey. Why did Godfrey perform better than Aloise by far?

You know that heavy dude at work or that fat workmate of yours who always starts talking about his/her dog or cat as soon as they arrive at work and before you know it, it's five o'clock afternoon and they are still talking about it. They don't do any work all day and the whole week goes on like that. These are the lazy ones. They neither work hard nor work smart. They spend most of their days gossiping about you. They are in their comfort zone and they never think of any change, let alone success beyond their current level. They are the first ones to get to work and the last ones to leave. Most of them are pessimistic as well. There is no idea you can share with them that they will say is going to succeed. However, they are always broke and they always have a long month at the end of their money.

Then there is this very hardworking skinny person in your workplace. This person is so hardworking that sometimes he/she forgets to go on breaks. They are always late in whatever they do which makes them be in a hurry every time. Time is never on their side. This person is so busy every day and every time so much that most of the times he/she carries some work home which eventually steals from him/her some good, healthy, much needed time with family, friends and enemies. Like the lazy ones, this hardworking dude of ours also has a very long month at the end of his money every month.

Everyone including yourself envies this well-shaped, physically, mentally, spiritually and the emotionally healthy lady who always has time to go to the gym before or after work and everyone borrows money from her. She drives one of those very beautiful latest cars and it's not on loan, work car lease scheme, or any of that drive now buy later schemes. She bought it by cash.

All this reminds me of this friend of mine whom I went to uni with. He and I did the same degree, Biomedical Sciences. His name is Graciano. He told me at uni that he wanted to work very hard and smart at the same time so that by the time he reaches 30 years old he would be a millionaire and he would never ever work for anybody again till he died. From the first month, he received his first paycheck when he was twenty one up to until he was twenty-six, he lived at his parents' home and saved $1,000 every month. After five years, his savings amounted to $60,000. By the time he reached thirty he had more than twenty houses rented out and his very beautiful house in which he still lives up to this day and each of his houses vomits at least $1,000 into his bank account every month. We are talking about at least $20,000 monthly income here. That's a dude who worked and is still working hard and smart.

We all know about how to be lazy. Everyone knows about how to work hard, even the extremely lazy ones, because that *"work hard for you to succeed"* song has been and is still being sung to us day and night by our teachers, our parents, our lecturers and our business mentors. Have you ever asked yourself: *"Why is it that everyone I know is working hard and earning the same salary and achieving the same results as everybody else, lazy people included?"*

What makes the difference is working smart. No matter how hard you work, you will never ever achieve the same things as a person who works smart in addition to working hard. It's the working smart thing that makes two people from the same background and earning the same salary and benefits have totally different levels of success in life whereby one can be financially broke and deeply in debt whereas the other one is already halfway to becoming a millionaire or a billionaire.

As well as working hard, anyone who wants to excel and be on top of the rest, be it at uni, at work or in business, must work smart. Working smart is a more profitable, beneficial and blessed way of working, not only money wise, but more so, physical, mental, spiritual, emotional and material wise.

This then leads us to this question; *What do smart working people do that others including hardworking people don't do?*

A very successful business friend of mine had this to say: *"If you want to be successful in anything in life you must work hard and work smart. It's the working smart part that's a sieve in people's lives. People who work smart are creative and they acquire life and time management skills. A very unique thing they do that separates them from the rest is that they provide scarce products and/or services to markets with a high demand. Not only are they very good at thinking before acting, carefully selecting the right opportunities, focusing on creating, delivering and capturing value, but they are also experts at innovating, being bold and having control. They also stand on the shoulders of giants. To them, networking is key and they play with people they can learn from."*

In my own study on this subject, I have also found out that timing is very crucial in life. If KFC, McDonald's, and Coca-Cola were to start their businesses today, they would be broke or liquidate soon after opening. They started their businesses during a very good time for them when people were oblivious to the detrimental effects of drinking fizzy drinks, eating high carbohydrate foods and eating fatty foods.

I have also found out that people who work smart write down a budget every month or every week depending on how they are paid and they write it down before they get paid and after getting paid they respect and follow it. In addition to this, they write down their short-term and long-term goals and work hard to achieve them. Whenever you see a smart working person working hard, he/she is working hard to achieve a goal within a set period of time.

Smart working people use the mastermind principle. A smart working friend of mine travels all over the world and never sleeps in a hotel or wastes money renting a house. She has got friends in all fields of work all over the world.

Smart working people are never comfortable in their comfort zone. That means they don't have a comfort zone. They are always hungry for change and change makes life more exciting and it also attracts opportunities.

If you study the lives of the most successful people in life, you will find out that in addition to working hard, they also work smart. When you study them further, you will find out that it's the working smart part that makes them only about 5% of the whole world's population. However, no matter how hard and smart they work, there is no guarantee for happiness because that precious free gift from GOD has its roots in the mind.

CHAPTER 5: Real Happiness in Life

Everyone wants to be happy including terrorists, criminals, Satanists, Christians, Muslims, Buddhists, Traditionalist, Atheists and even your enemies. Some spend years pursuing real happiness and others just take it as it comes without going out or in to look for it. What is real happiness? Where does it come from? How can you get it? When is it not real? Why do all people want it?

The Cambridge Advanced Learners Dictionary & Thesaurus defines happiness as *"the feeling of being happy."* They also define happy as *"feeling, showing or causing pleasure or satisfaction."*

After reading and understanding the meaning of happiness as defined by the dictionary, I went on to search what famous people, celebrities, philosophers, psychologies and theologians think happiness is and below is what I found:

"Happiness is when what you think, what you say, and what you do are in harmony."
— **Mahatma Gandhi**

"Happiness is not something ready made. It comes from your own actions."
— **Dalai Lama XIV**

"Happiness is a warm puppy."
— **Charles M. Schulz**

"It isn't what you have or who you are or where you are or what you are doing that makes you happy or unhappy. It is what you think about it."
— **Dale Carnegie**

"No medicine cures what happiness cannot."
— **Gabriel García Márquez**

"Happiness is having a large, loving, caring, close-knit family in another city."
— **George Burns**

"Of all forms of caution, caution in love is perhaps the most fatal to true happiness."
— **Bertrand Russell**

However, my own definition of happiness is, and I'm saying it aloud: *"Happiness is an emotion experienced in a state of well-being, contentment, pleasure, contentedness, satisfaction, cheerfulness, cheeriness, merriment, merriness, gaiety, joy, joyfulness, joviality, jollity, jolliness, glee, blitheness, carefreeness, gladness, delight, good spirits, high spirits, lightheartedness, good cheer, enjoyment, Felicity, exuberance, exhilaration, elation, ecstasy, delirium, jubilation, rapture, bliss, blissfulness, euphoria, beatitude, seventh heaven, cloud nine, humorous delectation or rare jouissance."*

From my own experience and research about happiness, I discovered that you are the only person who can make yourself happy and nobody else can. Everyone is busy trying to make themselves really happy so never blame anyone for not making you happy even Satan or GOD. Happiness is a free gift given by GOD to all human beings at birth without any form of discrimination and has its roots deeply embedded in everyone's mind.

Accumulation of wealth, riches, having a lot of money and/or material things do not mean you will be happy. In most cases, the more money and riches you accumulate, the more problems you attract and the more sad and unhappy you become. I have heard numerous stories of people who thought by having a lot of money they would be happy and they won the lottery and become suddenly rich, but, guess what, they filed for divorce, they are now sadder than before the money came in and some of them became ill or committed suicide.

Many people, you and I included, think that the current state of life they are in is not enough and it's what they don't have that will make them acquire real happiness. They are not satisfied with what they currently have. They never have gratitude. He marries Jane today and after a year or two, he thinks that Jane is not making him happy. They file for divorce and he marries Susan. He divorces again thinking that Susan is not making him happy and marries another woman again. What he does not know is that GOD never created all these women to bring happiness to him. His own happiness is within himself and GOD gave it to him for free at birth. The same thing applies to women as well.

People always crave for more. With what you already have right now, you can be really happy day and night if you know how. One day my six-year-old son said he was not happy because he did not have a dollar. I gave him a dollar and he said that it was not enough to buy the toy he wanted that cost $5 and now he was sadder. I gave him the $5 but this time, he no longer wanted the small toy that cost $5. He thought the bigger one that went for $8 would make him happy. I then taught him to be satisfied, happy and grateful for whatever he has in life without demanding or crying for more and all those other things would naturally flow to him. All adults do the same as my son did before I taught, trained and mentored him on happiness and gratitude.

If real happiness does not come from money, wealth, riches, other people (partners, friends and enemies included), animals, plants and material possessions, where does it come from?

This reminds me of my visit to Zimbabwe, one of the so-called poorest countries on earth. When I arrived at Mbare Bus Station in the capital city, Harare, everyone looked happy. They greeted me as though I was a friend or brother of theirs. Almost everyone had a smile on their faces and they laughed, talked and enjoyed life. On the bus from Harare to Masvingo, a three-hour journey, I talked to and made friends with fellow passengers starting with the person I shared a seat with to the people sitting on the other side and those behind and in front of me. You would think it was a big lovely family but we did not know each other and we had never met before.

I compared my experience in Africa to that I experience every day in developed countries like the United States of America and the United Kingdom. People share a bus seat for an hour or more and they never talk to each other. Some have never spoken to their neighbours and others don't even know how their neighbours look like. Although they are richer by far than the people in Africa, they all look stressed, depressed, sad, unhappy and miserable whereas the people in Africa share that very little they have got and are grateful for and happy with their lives. They are wealthy within.

Happiness is not outside of us but it's within us. It is deeply embedded within our brains and everyone has got it in an equal proportion no matter what colour of skin, race, physical ability, educational background, work experience or material wealth they do or do not own.

Jackson, a psychologist friend of mine told me: *"If you want to be happy starting from right now and keep on attracting happiness till you die, always think about past events, experiences, emotions, stories, films, videos and jokes that have made you laugh your lungs out in the past. You will always smile and people will think you are out of your mind because you will always be laughing, happy and smiling whereas they will be focusing on crying, sadness and misery. It's either you choose to be happy or you choose to be unhappy. The choice is yours. People can make you sad, unhappy and miserable, but no one will ever make you happy. They can only make you unhappy in the pursuit of their own happiness, but you must know that you are the only one responsible for switching on and off that real happiness button."*

A friend of mine, Moses makes sure he watches at least one funny video every day so that he can have some time to laugh no matter what. His friend's sister, Mary, meditates every night before going to bed and soon after the meditation, she gives herself half an hour to thinks about all the happy experiences of the day.

If you want real happiness, find a way of acquiring it by using your own mind, but first, you must be grateful for whatever and whomever you already have. Never take anything or anyone for granted and pester them to make you happy because the very day you lose them is the day you will realise that no one is responsible for making you happy except yourself. The only thing they can afford to do is making you sad and unhappy because they are also busy taking responsibility for their own happiness.

CHAPTER 6: How to sell anything to anyone anytime.

Do you know that you can sell anything to anyone anytime? Yes, you can! You not only need to have a deep understanding of your product, but more so, the customer you are selling it to. There are so many used clothes, used cars, used houses, dirty underwear, used furniture, to mention but a few, being sold for twice or even ten times more than they were worth when new. Are there no new ones? Are there no better ones? What extras do they have that make them special? Why do people buy them?

A close friend of mine recently bought extremely dirty shorts worn by David Beckham when his team Manchester United won the UEFA Champions League in 1999. Can you guess how much he bought it for? It was a huge five figure price for an extremely dirty used pair of shorts that probably were worth less than five dollars when Manchester United bought them new for their team. Why is that?

People buy because of emotion, not logic. Many times, they try by all means necessary to justify those emotions with logic. What are emotions? What is logic?

Collins English Dictionary describes emotion as: "a feeling such as happiness, love, fear, anger or hatred which can be caused by the situation that you are in, or the people that you are with."

Cambridge Dictionary describes logic as: "a particular way of thinking, especially one that is reasonable and based on good judgement."

People may buy your product for someone they love. They may buy it for themselves thinking it will make them happy or they may buy it because they fear that if they don't, they will miss out. Have you ever heard of the word FOMO (Fear Of Missing Out)?

Jealous makes people buy your products, too. The neighbor next door buys new beautiful sofas and the following day you receive an email from this marketer offering you more beautiful and cheaper ones than your neighbor's, your wife will convince you to buy them.

Anger and hatred may force people to buy your products. I know an old woman who bought an electric fence and put it around her house because she was angry about the neighbors' cats and dogs playing in her garden and destroying her flowers. An African cousin of mine hated mosquitoes and malaria so much that he bought a mosquito net.

The other thing you must know about your customers is that, they never buy into something so never ever try to sell anyone into anything no matter how good or beneficial it might be to them. They won't buy because anyone, even you and I included, never buy into something. You must understand and always keep it in your mind that people always buy their way out of something.

They buy food because they want to buy their way out of hunger. They buy drinks because they want to buy their way out of thirsty. They buy houses because they want to buy their way out of homelessness. They buy books because they want to buy their way out of ignorance. Why does this happen?

All this happens because of problems. People want to buy their way out of problems. Find a solution to a million people's problem and sell it for one dollar. Within less than a year you will be a multimillionaire. In other words, people want to buy solutions to their problems. Please always remember this whenever you buy something, no matter what it is, you are buying it because you have got a problem which you want to get out of, and you think that thing you are buying is a solution to the problem.

Why does a Mercedes-Benz E Class E220G AMG Line Premium 2dr 9G-Tronic used and driven by Lewis Hamilton for two or more years cost more than ten times a brand new one which costs only £37,498? Why does an extremely dirty pair of shorts worn by David Beckham during the game where Manchester United won the UEFA Champions League in 1999 cost more than a hundred times than a new one?

All this is because people don't buy products and/or services. People buy stories behind the products and services. In marketing and sales, we say: "Facts tell and stories sell." Whenever you are selling something to someone, always tell a story that pushes the customer's emotional buttons and then make them want to get out of their problem by buying your product or service.

Everyone has got a story. It may be a story about the history of the product, a story about the former owner of the product, a story about your own or your friend's experience of using the product, tell it but always make sure it is true and wherever there is proof, produce it. Have you ever asked yourself why people always go to the review section before they buy a product even if it is a very good product? They want to read the story.

People buy because of emotions. They never want to buy themselves into something, but they always want to buy themselves out of their problems. Facts tell and stories sell.

CHAPTER 7: How have you made money on the internet?

Last week, I took my wife and my son to dinner and on our way back home, my son asked me: "Why do you always take us out to dinner every first week of every month?"

I replied: "Because I write articles and stories on medium and get paid every first week of every month. That's how I make money on the internet?"

"Oh, My God!" He exclaimed and turned to his mom and whispered: "Mom, how have you made money on the internet?"

She answered: "Daily, you see me playing with the sewing machine your dad bought me as a birthday present. The real fact is, I'm not playing with it the same way you do with your toy dinosaurs. I make children's clothes with it and sell them on Etsy. I bought this car your dad is driving with the money I made on the internet."

As soon as we got home, my mobile phone rung. That was my cousin brother phoning me just to say "Hi" and have a chat with me. As soon as I pressed the green button to pick up the phone, my son shouted at the top of his voice: "How have you made money on the internet?"

By the way, my son is only seven years old.

Most people ask you this questions knowing or without knowing that they are not asking you the question they want to ask you. Nowadays everyone knows that people make money on Ebay, Amazon, Etsy, Medium, Shopify, Facebook, Youtube, Google, Quora, Warrior Forum, own blog or own website.

It's only when you make loads of money online, more money than your neighbors, friends and enemies that people start asking you: "How have you made money on the internet?"

Some people make money legally on the internet through; starting a blog, selling online courses on websites such as Udemy and Teachable, building an online community on Hittly, affiliate marketing using JVzoo, Clickbank, etc, writing stories, articles and poems on medium, and publishing Youtube videos.

There are so may other means and ways of making money on the internet that I have not included in the list above, for example, selling your ebooks on Amazon, etc.

There are so many opportunities these days, but there is too much competition, too. To survive, pay my bills and go on holiday, I use the MSI (Multiple Sources of Income) system.

The MSI system I use includes all the online income sources listed above. Imagine getting a passive income of at least $100 every month from Medium, then $50 from Youtube videos every month, $1000 from affiliate marketing every month, $250 from Udemy courses every month and another $50 from your blog. All that amounts to a total of $1450.

Even if I die today after reaching that far, money will keep on poring into my bank account for a long long period of time.

The question to you is:

How have you made money on the internet?

CHAPTER 8: Should you start up your own company or not?

Many people are confused. They don't know what they are good at, what they desire in life and what they believe in. Neither do they date themselves nor understand who they are.

"Before making any big decisions in your life, date yourself first." My mother used to tell me everyday when I was a kid.

There is a multi-drug resistant disease attacking most people these days. It's called the Fear Of Missing Out (FOMO).

You may see your friends and relatives starting up their companies and becoming successful and you think, *"May be I should start up a business as well and become prosperous like them."*

No. You better not. Life does not work like that. It's that FOMO disease starting to attack you. In life, if you do things just because everybody else is doing them, you end up being a loser.

Before starting up your own business, you should ask yourself these questions and write the answers in a notebook. Do I desire to run a business? If I become successful, how will I spend the money? Do I want to be successful? Is the type of business profitable? Is this the right time to start the business? Do I have enough capital? What has made other business fail? What lessons can I learn from their mistakes? How did the successful ones do it differently?

To start a business and become successful, you need to be self disciplined. That means you should have self mastery, self control, self responsibility and self direction.

Whenever something goes wrong you should be able to accept that it is your own fault then find out why and how it went wrong, learn from those mistakes and make corrections.

In addition to this, you should force yourself to do what you should do no matter how you feel. You should also be able to do things that the majority of people don't like to do. That's the price you must pay for the success you desire.

Furthermore, you should have integrity. You should be honest at all times no matter what. That is what makes people trust you and buy your products or services.

When I was a kid, my grandmother used to say to me, *"Never die until all your bones are rotten."*

Many people fail in business because they give up. They lack persistence or perseverance. Don't be like them. You should 'rise up every time you fall.'

Have you ever noticed that in life there are some people who don't write down clear specific short-term, medium-term and long-term goals. Like a ship without rudder, they just live without any sense of direction. If you are like them, you should change now before you start up your company.

Are you a doer? Prosperous business people are successful because they take action. They do not postpone, they do it there and then. However, they make sure everything that needs doing is done perfectly. They love the best quality.

Should you start up your own company or not? Yes, you should. However, you must date yourself first. Learn from others' and your own mistakes. Change the way you think about money. Make some changes in the way you live. Last but not least, acquire enough capital before you start.

CHAPTER 9: What are the most useful business startup ideas?

His flight from Puerto Rico to the Virgin Islands was cancelled. He hired a plane, rounded up all passengers who were supposed to be on the same plane with him to Virgin Islands, filled up his first plane and charged each passenger $39 one way to British Virgin Islands (BVI). That's how Sir Richard Branson started Virgin Airlines.

In the late 1970s there were no intercity coach services across Scotland. Whenever he visited Arthur Andersen's clients, Brian Souter noticed the non-existence of intercity bus services and the untapped demand with the expansion of the oil industry. The Stagecoach Group plc was founded in 1980 by Brian Souter, his sister Ann Cloag and her former husband Robin. It's a transport group based in Perth, Scotland. It operates buses, trains, trams and express coaches in the United Kingdom.

He read a report about the future of the internet. It projected an annual internet business growth of 2,300%. Jeff Bezos did his own research and found out that of all products that could be sold online, books were in demand, would sell quicker and would bring in more profit. Thus, Amazon was born.

If you clearly study all the businesses above and others including but not limited to: Microsoft, Facebook, Uber, AirBnB, Apple, Google, eBay, Alibaba, and PayPal, they share common things in the way they were born or got started. The people that started them share common personality traits as well.

The most useful business startup ideas may be inventions, innovations, disruptive or copycats, but the way they were born or created is almost the same.

Inventions are like this: you and your ancestors have been drinking water since life began. One hot summer day you are sitting under a tree holding your cup of hot water. Wind blows and leaves fall into your water. You drink the water after a minute or two and it tastes different. Everyday you boil these leaves in water and drink. The leaves happened to be tea leaves. You like the taste and the feeling you have after drinking it and you introduce it to friends, family and enemies. You have accidentally discovered and invented tea.

Someone with an innovative mind comes and adds sugar to your tea and sells it to other people. That person has just added something to a thing that was invented already.

AirBnB is the largest hotel business in the whole world but it does not own even a single hotel. Uber is the biggest taxi company in the world but it does not own taxis. Facebook is the biggest media company worldwide but it does not produce it's own content. When I say largest or biggest company I also mean in market capitalization and company share price. These are disruptive businesses.

What do all useful business startup ideas have in common?

All successful useful business startup ideas solve problems. People want solutions to their problems. They are always ready to buy themselves out of their problems. Thus, never come up with an idea that coerces people to buy into something. Rather come up with ideas that enable people to buy out of their problems. People want to live easy lazy lives. Find solutions to their problems and you are in big business.

I can hear you asking, *"So, how can I know people's problems?"*

Have a pocket size problem diary. On the first page, list your own problems. Be a problem man or woman by listing in your diary every problem in your house, at work, on the bus, on the train, in the toilet, and everywhere.

Decide on which problems you can solve and even if you can easily solve them, ask yourself, *"Am I passionate about it?"* If you are not, don't. Keep on searching until you find one you are passionate about.

Successful useful business startup ideas fulfill a lack of service or product in a particular area. Sir Richard Branson noticed the lack of a plane service from Puerto Rico to British Virgin Islands due to cancellation and he quickly hired a plane to fulfill that lack of service. Brian Souter noticed a lack of service and acted fast.

Furthermore, wherever and whenever people are complaining, there are business opportunities. Business opportunities come from people's complains. I would suggest that you have another pocket size diary called a complains diary. In it, write down every complain you hear at work, at home, in the shops, in the restaurants, on the train, on the bus and everywhere. These are all business opportunities waiting for you to take action.

In doing all this, always improve your knowledge by reading as many books as you can. Always learn, listen and ask questions. Never forget to innovate and challenge the status quo at all times.

In conclusion, I give you Sir Richard Branson's quotes:

"Business opportunities are like buses, there's always one coming." Sir Richard Branson.

"Do not be embarrassed by your failures, learn from them and start again." Sir Richard Branson.

"You don't learn to walk by following rules. You learn by doing, and by falling over." Sir Richard Branson.

CHAPTER 10: How can I start freelance writing fast without experience?

Sweat dripped down his forehead. It soaked the magazine he was reading. He took out a soiled handkerchief from his breast pocket, loudly blew his nose on it and used it to wipe sweat off his face, bold-head and chest.

The sweltering English summer of 2018 made John Socks lose a lot of water everyday. No matter how many liters he drank, he still lacked sleep and felt too weak to go to work. That first Monday of June 2018, he phoned in sick to work. He was a binman.

"What type of work can I do without getting out of bed too early and without anyone bossing me around? I know I am good at writing. Can I become a freelance writer? How can I succeed without any experience?" John asked himself as he switched the fan on.

It blew hot air into his face. He sneezed loudly, went to the bathroom and took a cold shower. With cold water running down his big fat body refreshing his skin, mind and emotions, he decided to phone his friend, Tim, an experienced freelance writer who makes a living writing for various publications all over the world.

"How are you John? How come you are not at work today?" asked Tim.

"I'm not feeling well. Anyway, I have been thinking. I want to start freelance writing but I don't know where to start. Can I be successful without any experience?" John responded.

"Yes you can. The best place to start as a newbie is Medium. Signup on Medium and join the Medium Partner Program. Make your stories, articles and poems eligible to earn money and allow curators to recommend your story to interested readers." Explained Tim.

He continued, *"To get many readers and claps for your articles, make them detailed, understandable and valuable to your readers. You should also publish in publications like: The Writing Cooperative, The Startup, Live Your Life On Purpose, The Butterfly, and many others. The advantage of doing this is that these publications have got hundreds of thousands of subscribers and your story is thrown right in front of their eyes. Besides that, they also email a newsletter featuring top stories of the week to all their subscribers."*

"Thank you for the advice, Tim." Said John.

*"John! John! Don't hang up, please. I have got more information for you. Have you ever heard of Steemit? It's a website where you can publish anything from pictures, videos, poems, articles to stories and you get paid depending on the

quality and quantity of up-votes you get. They pay you in a cryptocurrency called Steem which you can exchange for fiat currency on cryptocurrency exchanges." He added.

Tim drank a glass of ice-cold water and continued, *"There are also places where you can advertise your freelance writing skills and expertise and people will hire you to write small articles for them and pay you. I advertise my ad-copy writing skills on Fiverr and get paid $25 per 250 word article and everyday I get at least 5 orders. I also advertise my freelance writing skills on Upwork where I get at least 2 jobs per month. Sometimes I get paid $1000 per article, but these are very long articles or eBooks."*

"Oh! Oh! Oh my God! You make a lot of money, Tim!" Exclaimed John.

Tim responded, *"I treat every customer as a king and that makes them come back to me with their friends. Even if you start with one customer, never be discouraged. Just treat that customer as your king and he/she will come back to you and recommend you to friends, family and enemies."*

"Thank you for all this information. Are there any niche specific sites where I can publish my freelance work and get paid?" Asked John.

Tim answered, *"There is plenty of them. I will just mention them to you and then you do your own research about what type of articles they publish, who reads their publications and how much they pay you if they publish your article. They include: Photoshop Tutorials, Travel Writer's Life, Cracked, Treehouse, Tuts+ Code, Write Naked, International Living, Sitepoint, Metro Parent, A list Apart, Tuts+ Vector, Tuts+ WP, Digital Ocean, Smashing Magazine, and A Fine Parent."*

"Thank you, Tim. I am now starting a new career. Freelance writing it is." Said John.

Tim answered: *"You are welcome, John. We have had a long chat. I wish you good luck in your new career. Good bye!"*

"Bye!" John responded.

They both hang up their phones at the same time.

CHAPTER 11: What's the best online business to start that doesn't require much of an upfront investment?

Bongi had no money. He slept on the couch in his mom's house. His mom bought food and paid all the bills. Though he wanted to, he couldn't help her. He was unemployed and considered by many employers as unemployable. The gods were not smiling at him at all. But he was only 21.

A year ago, his dad had died of lung cancer. Although he had worked for 30 years as a fireman, he had not left anything for his beloved wife and only son except a one bedroom house and an old Hp Desktop computer and a Samsung smartphone.

Instead of pestering employers, Bongi decided to use everything he had to make a living. From the age of 13, he had been writing short stories and poems and saving them on his dad's computer.

After reading about Medium in the city council library, he decided to publish his writings on it and get paid for them through the Medium Partnership Program. He did so and after a year, he had earned about $10,000 dollars.

His best friend Donga was broke, too. Unlike Bongi, Donga was not a good writer at all. However, he always read books, magazines, and newspapers to improve his knowledge. One day he came across an article on affiliate marketing. He read it more than twice every day so that he could understand it and do exactly as it said.

With only a dilapidated laptop computer connected to his mom's broadband, he set up his affiliate marketing business. He started with products on Clickbank then went on to JVZoo and by now I think he is registered on more than ten affiliate marketing platforms.

He does not have a blog or website, but he builds landing pages on ClickFunnels and markets those landing pages. He then sends marketing emails to subscribers and gets sales.

Yesterday he showed me earnings of about $2000 per week for the past year. He says his main target is $5000 per week from the beginning of the second quota of 2019.

Donga's twin sister Danga makes a living buying and selling items on online marketplaces like eBay, Amazon, Etsy, and many others. She started with a laptop connected to the internet and $300 which she borrowed from her dad.

With just an iPhone his uncle bought him as a birthday present, Ethan recorded funny videos of himself playing with his dog and cat and uploaded them on YouTube. He monetized them so that he could earn money from advertisements displayed on them.

Although he started a year ago without any money, his YouTube channel now has more than half a million subscribers and each video he uploads gets more than 200,000 views within 48 hours.

Now that he also puts his affiliate marketing links in the description of every video, he now earns money from YouTube and from affiliate marketing. He is looking for a house to buy in one of the posh suburbs in Cheshire, England.

After being laid off work, my best friend, Martin never wanted to go back to a 9 to 5 job again. He used to work as a chef. Instead of looking for a job, he used his smartphone to make video tutorials of himself cooking different types of dishes and compiled them into courses with some useful notes attached. He sells them on Udemy.

Up to this day, he has made more than 20 courses and he is making a lot of money. In addition to this, he also writes recipe books and publishes them on Amazon.

There are so many people who make a living doing small jobs for other people and getting paid for that. They use websites like Fiverr and Upwork. They start with no capital at all.

However, in every type of business, be it online or offline, you should always treat every customer as king so that they can come back again and again and they can also recommend your business to their family, friends, and enemies.

CHAPTER 12: How do people become rich at a young age?

At exactly 04:00 am he left the house. In one hour, he walked three and a half miles. Yes, he walked too fast for his age. His strides were short, but at times he jogged. He was only ten years old.

His main aim was to get there before she woke up. *"She usually gets up at 05:00 am, cooks breakfast, eats, bathes and goes to work."* He said to himself as he walked. Panting and with his whole body socked to the bones in sweat, Ethan knocked on Mary's door.

Ethan had a very strong desire to run his own business. Though he was very young, everywhere he went, young and old people crowded around him like flies on fresh poo. This was because he was funny. Everything on and about him was funny. Every word that came out of his mouth was funny. That was food for them.

Ethan had watched all of Mary's Youtube videos and he wanted to learn from her. He wanted to find out how and why her videos were successfully getting more than sixty thousand views per day. In addition to that, he needed help on setting up his own Youtube channel. He also wanted to know how much Youtube paid per one thousand viewers.

"Ethan, you are a great person with so many talents. I am happy that you have come here to me to seek help and advice. I will help you." Said Mary.

Mary helped Ethan create a Youtube channel and he started uploading his funny videos. They included comedy, playing with pets and problem solving tips. As I write this answer, Ethan's Youtube channel has got more than two hundred thousand subscribers and he gets at least fifty thousand views on his new videos within twenty four hours of publication.

Now aged only twelve, Ethan earns more than $2000 every month from his Youtube videos alone and he is now planning to add affiliate marketing to his business as well.

To become wealthy at a young age, you should date yourself first before you date any girls or boys. During that self-date, please ask yourself the following questions and write the answers in a notebook you promise yourself to keep forever.

What am I good at? What are my talents? How can I make my talents and hobbies valuable to others? How can I solve other people's problems through using my own hobbies and talents? Who can help me and how can I approach him or her?

If you do things that you like and enjoy doing everyday, you will never be distracted. You will always focus. Mix them with your talents and your success is guaranteed.

CHAPTER 13: Can a religious blog be profitable?

He took a soiled handkerchief out of his torn breast pocket, sneezed on it and wiped off sweat from his face. It was a sweltering English summer, but Sam did not leave his house that day.

While everyone else was sat or walking nude at the beach, he was busy planning his new business venture. With all windows and doors open and the fan blowing hot air directly into his face, he built his blog using Wordpress.

His was a different type of blog. It was a religious one. He planned it in such a way that it would include many faiths without losing its main purpose of being funny, helpful, informative, problem solving and profitable.

"It's easy to make a religious blog funny, helpful, informative and problem solving, but how can I make it profitable?" He asked himself.

For a quick answer, he phoned me and asked me the same question.

I answered, *"First of all, you should put a donation button on your website so that people can donate money for the day to day running of the blog. After that you can then register with some Christian affiliate programs. On my list I have got ten."*

I continued, *"They include: Kerusso, DaySpring, Ignatius Press, The Jerusalem Gift Shop, Worship Guitar Class, BibleBelles, American Bible Society, Answers In Genesis, Trinity Road Websites, Nest Learning."*

"Thank you for the list. Besides affiliate marketing and a donation button, what else should I include?" Sam asked.

It wasn't his first time to setup and run a profitable blog. He asked many questions because this one was different. This was a religious blog and he was not a Priest, Monk, Pastor or Imam. He was just a devout Christian with unwavering faith in GOD.

"I know you are a devout Christian and you can write. Why not write a religious eBook and sell it on your blog?" I answered.

"Yes, that's a brilliant idea." said Sam.

I added, *"You can also create religious courses, put them on Udemy and market them on your blog."*

"Thank you for all these excellent ideas, Taka. See you soon," he said. We hang up.

When I last visited his website two days ago, I found out that he had also included an e-commerce store on his website where he sold antique religious goods like Bibles, relics and jewelry.

CHAPTER 14: How can I start making money on the internet?

It was excruciatingly cold outside. From my bedroom, with all doors and windows closed, I could hear the howling gale. It was dubbed, 'The Beast From The East.'

Some said it was caused by the collision (somewhere in Spain) of hot air from the Sahara desert and freezing air from the Atlantic ocean. Others called it a hurricane.

Although I did not get out of the house that day, I made a lot of money because my online businesses were not affected by the terrible weather.

"What do you do on the internet that makes you money?" I can hear some of you asking.

Well, it was five years ago when I started selling all goods that I didn't need. I sold them on eBay and within less than a week, I ran out of things to sell.

Every weekend, I visited car-boot sales, auction houses, and wholesalers in search of products to buy cheap and resell for a profit. I got a few and kept on doing it because money was flowing into my pockets.

It became addictive and I started buying Amazon customer returns, shop customer returns and liquidation goods on liquidation websites.

In addition to selling on eBay, I also sold on Amazon and my own website. I also added drop-shipping to the business. Most of the drop-shipped products were bought on Alibaba.

Furthermore, I also had a hobby of making jewelry. Instead of selling it on eBay, Amazon and my own website, I sold it on Etsy. Etsy is a good online marketplace for selling handmade items that you make yourself. I am still doing that.

One Sunday afternoon in 2017, my old friend Sam asked me, *"Do you know that you can make a lot of money selling valuable products without storing them, dealing with customer complains and returns and without a website?"*

"How?" I asked.

"It's called affiliate marketing, mate. It's a type of selling retailers' goods and services on the internet and they pay you a commission for sales generated from your referrals." He replied.

On that same day, I registered an account with Clickbank and another one with JVzoo. I then watched videos on Youtube on how to do affiliate marketing without a website.

That's how I got knowledge about how to make a landing page using ClickFunnels, how to use an email auto-responder like Mailchamp and Aweber, how to build an email list, and how to market on Youtube, Facebook, Quora and also how to get leads from solo ads.

It was at the beginning of the second quota of 2018 that my friend, Graciano, told me, *"I am making at least $500 per month writing and publishing my short stories, articles and poems on Medium. You can, too. Make sure after registering you join the partner program to get paid."*

Publishing my stories, articles and poems on Medium now pays all my monthly household bills. I now no longer write them myself. I hire people on Fiverr to write them for me and I pay them a small fee.

By the way, I also make money by doing small jobs for people on Fiverr. I use my talents, knowledge and expertise to help others and to solve others' problems and I get paid for it.

Youtube pays people who allow it to show adverts on their videos. If you are interested, you can checkout their rules and regulations about this on their website.

In January this year, my son asked me, *"Dad, why don't you compile your videos into a course and sell it on Udemy?"*

I asked, *"What?"*

"Yes, my friend's dad is doing it with his fitness videos. He uploads some on Youtube, but the ones he does not put on Youtube are for a Udemy course. He makes more than a thousand dollars per month," he answered.

I now sell my courses on internet marketing on Udemy and I am also planning to write an eBook, publish it on amazon and market it myself.

CHAPTER 15: How do small businesses get Instagram and twitter followers?

Many people go on twitter and Instagram with the aim of getting followers. They only get a few or none and quit.

"This doesn't work. You have to be a celebrity or some rich person of some sort to get followers." They will tell you.

They are lying.

The number one reason why they fail to get followers is because they go on Instagram and twitter looking for followers. There are no followers.

All there is on Instagram and twitter are people who want to feel important, be happy and escape from their problems, insecurities, lack of confidence, stress and anxiety.

If you have ever taken a walk in the forest you know that if you start giving food to birds, they will follow you for as long as you keep feeding them.

People on Instagram and twitter are like birds and you are the person taking a walk. They will never follow you unless you give them something they want, need or like.

You can achieve this by identifying your talents and hobbies first. Take those related to your specific target niche market and then find out how you can make them valuable to other people in a unique way.

"How can I make a talent or hobby valuable?" Some of you are asking.

Ethan spend a year taking funny photos and videos of himself and his dog and cat and upload them on Instagram before he started his affiliate marketing business. Now he has got more than one hundred thousand followers and he is selling pet food, pet clothes and many items for pets to his followers.

People watching his pictures and videos laugh, cry, scream, and some have even admitted wetting their pants.

Thus, you should give valuable content to people and they will follow you. Valuable content is that which arouses people's emotions, for example, laughter, crying, love, happiness, joy, to mention but a few.

It's also that type of content which gives a lot of that much needed important information and help to people. Bring solutions to people's problems and they will follow you like you are a god.

Whenever people hear, read about, see or watch something, the first question that their own minds ask themselves subconsciously in many times is, *"What's in it for me?"*

Everyone wants to feel important even you and me. If you make a person feel important, that person will follow you.

I can hear you asking again, *"How do I make people feel important?"*

Dish out genuine complements to them, make them tell you about themselves instead of you telling them about yourself, ask them questions so that they feel intelligent and knowledgeable, and never forget to always be generous with the truth about yourself and your own opinions.

Please, in whatever you do, remember that people always follow people who bring solutions to the table not problems.

CHAPTER 16: How do people become successful?

Ethan loves winning. In everything he does, he always wants to be number one. If he doesn't win, he plays that game again, repeats that crossword puzzle, enters that competition again until he wins.

That doesn't mean he never loses. However, he always rises up each time he falls. He never gives up and he will work day and night, get advice from experts, read books about it, and learn it until he comes up tops. It may be school work, a game, a competition, a new life challenge, or anything in life.

One day he took part in an online computer game competition, got second place and won a Samsung smartphone. The number one person won the same Samsung smartphone and $5 worth of airtime, but Ethan cried and got angry with himself that he didn't become number one.

He spend a month playing that same game over and over again everyday and entered the same competition again. This time he became number one. Though there wasn't much difference between the number one and second place prizes, Ethan was over the moon just because he had won the first place.

Besides loving and enjoying winning, Ethan is a very successful man. He runs five prosperous businesses two of which earn him a passive income. Hitherto, he has got more than one hundred million dollars in his bank account.

Successful people are supper competitive. They are so because they love and enjoy winning. That does not mean they never lose. Whenever they lose, they learn lessons from that loss, acquire more knowledge from books and experts so that they can win next time, and they keep on competing without loss of enthusiasm.

If you change your life now and become supper competitive in everything you do in life you will see your life making some drastic positive changes and moves towards success. Competition makes capitalism what it is.

Besides being supper competitive, Ethan never leaves anything he starts unfinished. If he starts writing a book, he makes sure he writes it from the beginning to the end within the exact amount of time he scheduled for himself. Whenever he starts a project, be it a software program, a computer game, or a business venture, he makes sure he completes it.

Successful people always finish things. Whatever they start doing, they make sure they complete it. Even if it's something boring or tedious, they still finish it. If you want to be successful in your life, make sure you finish every project, course of study, book, business venture, competition, or challenge you start. Never leave anything unfinished.

Although he is a very friendly person, Ethan always surrounds himself with people that are smarter than him, more successful than him, more competitive than him, wealthier than him, more hard-working than him and more optimistic than him.

His circle of friends, acquaintances, competitors and enemies earn him money, knowledge, skills, expertise, experience, let alone the will to succeed.

Successful people play with people who are smarter than them. They make friends with people who are richer, cleverer, and more successful than them. If you want to be successful starting from now, choose and play with the type of friends that successful people do.

Furthermore, Ethan is always thinking about solving problems. Even when in bed he thinks about how he can make his clients and customers happier, how his businesses can take advantage of Brexit, when he can buyout his competitors, what can make him win the next competition, how to start and complete his next project and many other things.

The mind of a successful person never stops. If you want to be successful, please always think about how you can solve people's problems. There are so many problems in everyday life. Identify them and solve them. People will love you. All businesses, innovations and inventions are built to solve people's problems. It's big business.

Although he is a successful man, Ethan is always reading books. He reads and finishes at least one book per week. Whenever he is watching telly or videos on YouTube, he is gaining some education from them. You will never see him watch a movie that makes him cry, sad, nervous, anxious, scared or afraid. Once everyday he watches something funny that makes him lough for at least thirty minutes.

Successful people are always learning. They read books, they write books, they learn from their coaches and students, they learn from their customers, they learn from their clients and they learn from friends, family member and enemies.

If you want to be successful, you should be always learning. Learning from everyone, even your kids.

Moreover, successful people are obsessive. If you want to be successful, copy them and success will be yours.

By the way, success is the achievement of a purpose, aim or goal.

CHAPTER 17: The Growth Stages of Venture-Backed Private Companies.

If you would have bought $1,000 worth of Facebook shares at its initial public offering (IPO) and held on to them until today, with a price of $205.12 as of December 24, 2019, your 26 shares would now be worth $5,333.12 which is more than 5 times (5x) your initial investment.

Now, imagine how much your $1,000 investment would be worth today if you had invested it during the early stages of the company. You would be a multi-millionaire by now.

Facebook, Inc. was founded by Mark Zuckerberg, Andrew McCollum, Dustin Moskovitz, Eduardo Saverin and Chris Hughes in Cambridge, Massachusetts, United States of America (USA) in February 2004. It went public with its IPO on May 18, 2012 with a share price of $38. Thus, it became open for the general public to invest in it more than eight years after it was founded.

Why do companies spend years before they can be bought by or merged with bigger companies, or undergo an initial public offering? How do companies grow? What are the growth stages of a company? When do companies start paying dividends to investors?

From inception and initial funding to exit by either mergers and acquisitions (M&A) or initial public offering, venture-backed private companies undergo four stages of growth which include:

(1) The angel or early stage.

(2) The mid stage.

(3) The late stage.

(4) The exit stage.

If you invest your money during any of these stages, you have got a high chance of getting a huge return on investment and a high chance of getting very little or zero. These are very risky stages, that is why they are not open to the public. They are only open to accredited investors.

To be an accredited investor, you must have a net worth of at least $1 million, excluding the value of your primary residence. Or you must have an annual income of at least $200,000 for the last two years (or at least $300,000 in combined annual income if married) and have the expectation to make the same amount for the current year.

Early stage:

The angel or early stage is that stage when the business is in the start-up phase and it focuses on research and development (R&D), proof of concept, product or service creation, and securing early rounds of capital, usually from angel or early seed investors.

An angel investor is also known as a private investor, seed investor or angel founder and it's a person who provides capital to a start-up business in exchange for convertible debt or ownership equity. Some of the early stage investors could be family, friends and enemies.

They invest in the founders, big inventions, innovations, or disruptive ideas. The business may have no product or an early product, and no or low revenue.

Companies in this growth stage have got a high cash burn rate, and failure rates of 40% to 60%.

If you invest during the early stage you have got the biggest return potential since you can buy a very high percentage of the company's equity cheap.

However, companies in this stage show huge losses and negative net cash flows because they spend a lot on early versions of the product, team infrastructure, and market growth. This stage is also the riskiest stage to invest your money in, but, mind you, the higher the risk, the more the return on investment if the project becomes successful.

Mid stage:

After the early stage, a company goes into the mid stage. In this stage, the company refines it's business model, captures the market share, and starts to generate revenue. The business now has revenue streams of between $10 million and $50 million or more with growth rates of in excess of 100% per year.

Investing in a company in its mid stage of growth has lower risk than investing in an early stage company because the failure rate in the mid stage is lower than in the early stage.

The risk of investing in a company that is in the mid stage of growth comes from substantial cash burn needed to achieve and maintain high growth levels, and the level of inherent execution risk.

Late stage:

Most companies in the late stage of growth are making revenues more than $50 million with growth rates of 25% to 50% or more per year.

This is the stage when a business does incremental product improvements, grows its market share, and has a strong focus on maintaining its market share if total market growth is slowing.

The likelihood of a late-stage company failing falls as the customer base, product line, and revenue grow. A business in this stage is now moving closer to an exit which may either be a merger or acquisition, or an initial public offering.

High net worth individuals and venture capitalists who are keen on lowering their risk and increasing their return on investment at the same time, invest in companies that are in the late stage and some of them get more than 80% success rates.

Exit stage:

Businesses exit through a merger with another company, an acquisition by a bigger company, for example, the sale of Instagram and its 13 employees to Facebook for $1 billion in cash and stock in April 2012.

Most companies in the exit stage focus on extending their market share. They now have got revenue levels of $200 million or more with average annual growth rates of 10% to 25%.

These companies now have huge exit expenses and legal complexities depending on the type of exit route the want to follow.

If it's an exit through an IPO, investors putting in their money during this stage carry lock-up risks on their backs. Lock-up is a risk because of a combination of illiquidity and general market volatility.

Most IPO lock-up last for 180 days following the offering which is a very long time if you are someone who wants to quickly get in and get out as soon as possible like someone having a cold shower.

Conclusion:

Venture-backed private companies follow the J Curve during their life cycle. At first they put in negative revenue and profit in their initial post-launch years, but then start witnessing gains after they find their footing. Although investing in private companies still undergoing the four stages of growth is too risky, and not accessible to the general public, the returns on investment can be very huge and in some cases a $1,000 investment was turned into more than $1 million. My next story will show you how you and me can now invest small amounts of money we can afford to lose in these companies without us being required to be high net worth individuals or venture capitalists.

CHAPTER 18: Now you can play ball.

Before the fifth of April 2012, you and me couldn't play ball. Not only were we boxed out, but more so, we were not even allowed nearby.

On 5 April, 2012, the then president of the United States of America, Mr Barack Obama, signed the Jumpstart Our Busness Startups (JOBS) Act that loosens regulations instituted by the Securities And Exchange Commission (SEC) on small businesses.

In addition to lowering reporting and disclosure requirements for companies with less than $1 billion in revenue, <u>it allows greater access to crowd-funding and greatly expands the number of companies that can offer stock without going through SEC registration.</u>

Before the signing of this act, only acredited investors like venture capitalists and high net worth individuals were allowed to invest in startup and/or private companies.

<u>Wikipedia describes venture capital (VC)</u> "as a type of financing that is provided by firms or funds to small, early-stage, emerging firms that are deemed to have high growth potential, or which have demonstrated high growth (in terms of number of employees, annual revenue, or both). Venture capital firms or

funds invest in these early-stage companies in exchange for equity, or an ownership stake, in those companies."

To be an accredited investor, you must have a net worth of at least $1 million, excluding the value of your primary residence. Or you must have an annual income of at least $200,000 for the last two years (or at least $300,000 in combined annual income if married) and have the expectation to make the same amount for the current year.

Now the general public including you and me can invest in startup and/or private companies, thanks to President Barack Obama's signing of the JOBS act. Hitherto, there are so many platforms where you can invest in startup businesses.

If you have got a brilliant invention, an excellent innovetion or a big disruptive business idea, you can also register on these platforms and get your business funded by venture capitalists, high net worth people and the general public. The platforms include:

(1) Companisto.

(2) Seedrs.

(3) Crowdcube.

(4) Funders Club.

(5) Ourcrowd.

(6) Onevest.

(7) Gust.

(8) Wefunder.

(9) Angel Kings.

(10) Seedinvest.

You can also advertise and/or pitch your startup company on these platforms and get funding.

CHAPTER 19: 20 Jobs You Can Do With Just General Certificate of Secondary Education (GCSE) Qualifications:

Tears flooded his eyes. He read the results slip for the third time and started crying loudly. Tears ran in rivulets down his cheeks and dropped onto the sunbaked ground suddenly evaporating like first drops of rain in a desert.

John had dismally failed his GCSEs. He only had a C in Maths, a C in English and a C in Geography. All the other seven subjects were below grade D.

"I don't qualify to go for "A" Level and that means I will never get a well-paying job," he thought as he slowly walked home.

That was five years ago and now, John is a Head Chef in a five-star hotel in London and he earns more than £30,000 per annum, thanks to his diligence, enthusiasm, and the will to succeed.

So many people think that if they have got only GCSEs or no GCSEs at all they won't be successful in life. They are wrong. Besides starting your own business, there are so many jobs that you can get even if you only have GCSEs or less as your highest qualification. Below are twenty of them:

Sale Executive:

Sales executives are responsible for all the sales activities of a company. They introduce, demonstrate and sell products to customers or clients, and they also make sure customers are satisfied with the products or services.

If you enjoy talking to people and getting on with them, this job is for you. Your communication skills could take you far.

The starting salary is about £20,000 per annum and after some years of experience you could earn up to £35,000 per year.

Entry requirements are usually two or more GCSEs at grade C or above. There are apprenticeships available, too.

Plumber:

If you enjoy fitting and repairing the pipes, fittings and other apparatus of water supply, sanitation, or heating systems, this job is for you.

Plumbers' salaries range between £31,200 and £36,400. Entry requirements are GCSEs at grade C or better in English and Maths. There are also some apprenticeships available.

As a plumber, there are high opportunities for you to start your own company and become self-employed and/or employ other plumbers to work for you.

Builder:

There are always houses and other buildings that need repairing, or building. Builders are always needed even during a recession.

To start training as a builder you only need to have at least 3 GCSEs at grade C or higher and there is a lot of apprenticeship positions available.

As a builder, you can earn from £20,000 to £35,000 per year depending on your experience and the company you are working for.

You can get more details about the qualifications, training, and apprenticeships on the City& Guilds website.

Customer Service Representative:

They are in the sales and marketing industry and their salary ranges from £20,280 to £30,000 per year. Usually, there are no set entry requirements which mean if you are a people person you can get the job without any GCSEs.

Estate Agent:

If selling and renting out buildings and land for clients is what you want, you should become an estate agent.

Entry requirements are five GCSEs at grade C or better usually including English and Maths. There are also apprenticeship positions available.

Estate agents earn between £22,800 and £70,000 depending on experience, niche and company worked for.

Forensic Computer Analyst:

Forensic computer analysts investigate all kinds of cybercrime from online child abuse to terrorism. The jobs are in the digital industry and you may start as an apprentice. Entry requirements are five GCSEs at grade C or higher including English and Maths.

Salaries start from £20,000 per annum and can go up to £60,000 depending on experience and how hard-working you are.

Other:

Other jobs you can get with only GCSEs as your highest level of education include:

Firefighter (Salary range: £34,840 to £50,000 per annum).

Army Officer (Salary range: £28,000 to £102,000 per annum).

Head Chef (Salary range: £16,000 to £35,000 per annum).

Pilot (Salary range: £101,400 to £120,640 per annum).

Fitness Manager (Salary range: £28,000 to £34,000 per annum).

Site Manager (Salary range: £27,000 to £70,000 per annum).

Driver (Driving HGV trucks, Buses or trains. Salary range: £15,000 to £40,000 per annum).

Receptionist (Salary range: £12,000 to £16,000 per annum).

Accounts Clerk (Salary range: £12,000 to £16,000 per annum).

Medical Secretary (Salary range: £14,834 to £21,318 per annum).

Waiting staff (Salary range: £11,000 to £14,500 per annum).

Healthcare Assistant (Salary range: £12,000 to £16,000 per annum).

Care Assistant (Salary range: £12,000 to £16,000 per annum).

Engineering Maintenance Fitter (Salary range: £15000 to £30000 per annum).

The fact that you don't have or you only have GCSEs as your highest qualification does not mean the end of the world. If you are hardworking, enthusiastic and willing to learn you can succeed. Mind you, success is the achievement of your own goals not others'.

CHAPTER 20: How to Revive Your Business After Lockdown

Many businesses closed in early 2020 when governments worldwide introduced lockdown to stop the spread of Covid 19 by disrupting the chain of transmission.

During the lockdown, business costs keep pilling up in the form of rentals, salaries and many others without any revenue. By the time the lockdown comes to an end, many small and medium businesses will have no cash left to continue operating. They will close forever.

The European Centre for Disease Prevention and Control says, *"Severe Acute Respiratory Syndrome Coronavirus-2 (SARS-CoV-2) is the name given to the 2019 novel coronavirus. COVID-19 is the name given to the disease associated with the virus. SARS-CoV-2 is a new strain of coronavirus that has not been previously identified in humans."*

Wikipedia describes a lockdown as: *"an emergency protocol that usually prevents people or information from leaving an area."*

In this article, we are going to explore ways of reviving your business after lockdown so that you may keep running it profitably and not close for good.

Identify the Problem:

"What do you mean by 'identify the problem' when everybody knows the problem is the lockdown," I can hear many of you saying that to yourselves.

Businesses are not affected in the same way by this same situation. A pub down the street that was closed last month is expected to pay salaries to workers and pay rent even though it's not open. It will soon run out of cash. Thus, when all the quarantine or lockdown ends, the pub will reopen but with cash flow problems it never had before.

The dressmaking business in town closed the same day the pub down the street did and also incurs the same rental and salary costs as the pub. However, all the workers are working at home making dresses, and disposable face masks, and selling them online during quarantine. When lockdown ends, they won't have the same cash flow problems as the pub. I'm not saying they won't have problems. Theirs will be different.

Therefore, it's very important to identify the problems. Write them on a piece of paper and look for workable and doable solutions.

Don't be afraid and never have pride:

After identifying all your business problems, please admit that there are huge problems in your business and show genuine humility. Doing this will help your mind to become open to advice, new ideas, and change.

Willingness to make some changes is a difficult gift to obtain especially to those who are fearful and/or proud. To humble people, it's an easy blessing from God. Don't be afraid of failure. Make as many mistakes as you can and also learn from each and everyone of them.

"Failure is one of the secrets to success, since some of the best ideas arise from the ashes of a shuttered business." — Richard Branson.

Know your customers or clients:

To succeed in business, you don't sell what you feel like selling, but you sell what the customers want and/or need. Go on social media, for example, Facebook, Instagram, LinkedIn and Twitter to find out what your customers are looking for and what your competitors are doing.

Don't be shy to ask for referrals. The foundation of every business is trust. People trust their friends, family, associates, and enemies more than advertisements and salesmen.

Re-market your products and services to your current and past customers. 80% of your business comes from 20% of your customers. Please, make them keep coming back to your business for more.

Your employees:

Fire that dude whom you pay $1500 per month for doing a job that you can easily get done by someone you can hire on Fiverr and save more than $1000 per month.

Automate that repetitive task done by ten people you pay $15000 per month and save more than $10000 per month.

That store keeper you are paying $1300 per month can be fired today and you start selling your products online. You will save more than $1300 every month.

However, you must keep talented, experienced, and hardworking workers because they are the backbone of your company. Never lose talented workers. Complement them daily and pay them handsomely.

Cut costs:

If you can do all your business from home and online, why keep on renting an office? Fire your landlord and work from home. Convert that attic, small bedroom or garage into your office the same way you did during lockdown and save money.

Make a list of all your business costs and reduce or get rid of them so that your business can survive.

Make your assets bring in money:

"Oh! My business is collapsing what should I do? The banks are not lending me any money," I can hear many of you crying.

Why are you not renting out some of the rooms in you business premises? Don't sell the building. Occupy space that is enough for your business and rent out the extra space to other businesses. You should also rent out some of your machinery and make money.

Conclusion:

Last but not least, be open to ideas and seek advice, for example, by engaging a professional business consultant to help you revive your business.

CONCLUSION:

Their aim was to connect Harvard University students through an online community. They ended up creating the biggest media company that does not produce its own content. It now has more than 1.6 billion worldwide users.

Mark Zuckerberg, Eduardo Saverin, Andrew McCollum, Dustin Moskovitz, and Chris Hughes founded Facebook and changed the way people socialize, share, do business, and communicate with workmates, acquaintances, family, friends, and enemies. Today, Facebook, Inc. is one of the big five technology companies along with Microsoft, Amazon, Apple, and Google.

However, Facebook and its founders are not the only ones with this distinguishing quality or characteristic that makes everyone with it successful.

The hotel industry is running scared of a big hotel company that's taking a huge chunk of the hotel business, but this company does not own even a single bed and breakfast, let alone a hotel.

In August 2008, Brian Chesky, Nathan Blecharczyk, and Joe Gebbia founded Airbnb. It disrupts the hotel industry by providing an online marketplace for people to rent out their properties or spare rooms to guests.

The same success trait is in many other businesses and their founders, too. For example, Uber Technologies, Inc., commonly known as Uber has got more than 110 million worldwide users. Travis Kalanick and Garrett Camp founded Uber in March 2009 and up to this day, it is the biggest taxi company in the whole world but it does not own even a single taxi.

All the people and companies mentioned above owe their success to doing things differently. Some people call it innovation and others call it disruption. Doing things differently is changing the way things are normally, traditionally, or always done.

Sheldon Gary Adelson, an American business magnate, investor, philanthropist, and political donor once said: *"If you do things differently, success will follow you like your shadow, and you can't get rid of it."*

Many people are scared of change. It puts you into the unknown and threatens your security. Not only does it take you out of your comfort zone, but sometimes it may present itself as a problem. However, the two worst enemies of change are the very two worst enemies of success and they are comfort and experience.

Comfort makes you scared of change. Daily, it serenely whispers into one of your ears, *"Just stay in your comfort zone. If you do things differently, you will never be as comfortable as you are right now. Never change anything."*

Into the other ear, experience whispers in support of comfort, *"You know that last time when you tried to do things differently you failed dismally. Never try it again. Didn't that experience of failure hurt you? Why do you want to persist? Why do you want to change things? You are good as you are, and never try to do anything differently. Just do things the same way you and your ancestors have been doing them since birth."*

John Davison Rockefeller Sr. once said: *"If you want to succeed, you should strike out new paths, rather than travel the worn paths of accepted success."*

My neighbor is a heavy dude. Before the Covid-19 pandemic, he went to and from work by bus every day. Now, because he is scared of using public transport, he jogs the 1.5-mile journey to work and walks back home every day. He works at the local hospital. So far, he has lost more than 15Kg and has been doing that for only one month. He is now enjoying the benefits of losing weight and many people are admiring him because he is doing things differently.

Doing things differently or changing the way things are normally, traditionally, or always done does not only apply in business, but it also applies to every person's daily life. If you want to succeed in life, make sure you introduce at least one positive change to your life every day and within a week you will start noticing some improvements, and little success miracles in your life.

DISCLAIMER

(1) *All content found in my articles, including text, images, audio, or other formats were created for informational purposes only and is not financial advice. The Content is not intended to be a substitute for professional financial advice.*